T0380985

The American Dream Come True

SIGRID CARTER

Order this book online at www.trafford.com
or email orders@trafford.com

Most Trafford titles are also available at major online book retailers.

 www.trafford.com

North America & international
toll-free: 844 688 6899 (USA & Canada)
fax: 812 355 4082

Our mission is to efficiently provide the world's finest, most comprehensive book publishing service, enabling every author to experience success. To find out how to publish your book, your way, and have it available worldwide, visit us online at www.trafford.com

Because of the dynamic nature of the Internet, any web addresses or links contained in this book may have changed since publication and may no longer be valid. The views expressed in this work are solely those of the author and do not necessarily reflect the views of the publisher, and the publisher hereby disclaims any responsibility for them.

Any people depicted in stock imagery provided by Getty Images are models, and such images are being used for illustrative purposes only.
Certain stock imagery © Getty Images.

ISBN: 978-1-6987-0747-1 (sc)
ISBN: 978-1-6987-0748-8 (e)

Print information available on the last page.

Trafford rev. 08/28/2024

The American Dream Come True

Written with a German Accent

Dedication

"Alabama," Pfc. Earl C. Bouldin
1928-1952

Sigrid dedicates every 4th of July to Pfc. Earl C. Bouldin of DeKalb County, Alabama, who lost his life fighting for our freedom during the Korean War, June 1950 to July 1953. It was a brutal war between Freedom and Communism. North Korea and China were backed the Soviet Union, South Korea was backed by the United States of America. Roughly 33,385 U.S. soldiers lost their lives so that we can live in freedom and enjoy life under capitalism, based on the U.S. Constitution and under the protection of God's 10 commandments.

On April 10, 1952, Holy Thursday, "Alabama" mentioned that all during the night he had felt uneasy about the day ahead. Later that morning as he and his team was dealing with a booby-trapped hut, they recommended, "just leave it, and search for a less dangerous place." "No," Alabama replied, "it would not be right to leave the hut that way to kill someone else." That evening, after Alabama's death, Alabama received his rotation orders, having served his nine months of combat in Korea.

Another great U.S. soldier is Thomas Sowell, a hero of African heritage who served as a Marine in Korea. He grew up in Harlem, New York, did not finish High School, and joined the Marines. Following his military service, he applied to and was admitted to Harvard University. Today Dr. Thomas Sowell is one of the U.S.A.'s prominent economists, and famous newspaper columnists.

What makes the 4th of July the second most celebrated holiday on earth?

It is men's natural passion for independence, freedom, equality, and the pursuit of happiness.

A man's character is his fate!

-*Heraclitus*

*True freedom is closely tied to living
a just and virtuous life*

-Plato

Sigrid's first American Independence Day

Happy facts about Fourth of July

It's man's natural passion for FREEDOM that makes the 4th of July the second most celebrated holiday on earth. No matter which country I visited in my exciting job as tour escort, the 4th of July was party time. Pockets of Citizens of the United States of America, left behind by wars, peace, and love were found celebrating on the 4th of July. There would be US Fags, Barbeques, cool lemonades, enthusiastic singing of the United States' National Anthem, ***"Oh say can you see, by the dawns early light...,"*** and yes, there would be an unbelievable outpouring of love for the Unites States of America by people from around the world, reminding me that Americans are the most appreciated people on earth.

On the days prior to the big celebration the spirit among the residents of our small town of Ransom Canyon, Texas ran at an all time high. Lawns were being groomed, trees pruned, porches dusted, and sidewalks swept. On our "party island" volunteers piled up firewood for the big B.B.Q. And John spruced up the banner for his once a year enterprise, "Fireworks! Buy 1 get 1 Free." At number 8 East Lakeshore Drive, across the street, our neighbors polished their antique Ford and decorated it with flags and streamers, in red, white and blue, of course. And Dr. Wood, our house guest from back east, the history professor, reminded us,

"The first Independence Day Celebration was held July 2, 1777 in Philadelphia. Bells rang all day, festive bonfires flamed in the streets, special dinners were held, politicians gave speeches, soldiers paraded and fireworks sparkled. But, amidst all the fun and celebrations they did not forget the great sacrifices men, women and children endured in order to give us this wonderful nation. Let us always remember the terrible battles, and the many lives it took to achieve the freedom we enjoy today."

He paused respectfully. He mused, as if his mind saw all the gunfights, the burning homes and forts, the ships swallowed by the sea and the fireworks of the past. Then he asked, "And what major event took place July Fourth 1803 ?" The professor's piercing blue eyes nailed us into our rocking chairs on the breezy, lakeside dock We gazed at each other dumbfounded and coaxed him into giving us more information. He fueled our wild guesses with remarks like, "The historic event that took place July Fourth 1803 more than doubled the size of our nation."

"The Louisiana Purchase! Yes, of course. On July Fourth, 1803, Napoleon sold the land west of the Mississippi for 3 cents an acre to Jefferson. The largest land deal ever made, it reached from the Mississippi to the Rockies, from Canada to Mexico." Julia, a student of Dr. Wood, cheered. Dr. Wood closed his eyes and smiled as if listening to Beethoven. Julia asked,

"Who among us here today has celebrated the most humorous Fourth of July?"

I gave it a shot, "The year we moved to West Texas we celebrated the Fourth of July with some 'Limies' in Lubbock. We teased them and didn't let them forget that they had nothing to celebrate since they lost America on July Fourth. They handled nagging rather well, with royal dignity, I thought. With their candid British humor they joked about losing the America colonies and asked us. "All right Gringos, anyone here at the party knows what our King George wrote in his diary July Fourth 1776?"

With a professor's voice Dr. Wood quickly replied. "The King of England wrote in his daily notes, "Today, nothing important happened."

Quickly the Limies protested, "Of course, that's what the vicious media says."

Looking for a gracious way out Dr. Wood focused on the ice in the tall Coca Cola glass filled with Gatorade. Ice-spoon in hand, he reached into the ice-bucket on the round table in front of him. He took an ice cube and placed it on his head underneath his large sombrero. Then he dipped again into the reservoir of his knowledge and stated…"And in 1854 Rowland Macy of Haverhill, Massachusetts, organized a Fourth of July parade. Mr. Macy's intention was to lead customers from the popular shoppers paradise of Haverhill across town to his deserted and ailing shop. He hired an eight-piece marching band and a orator who was to deliver a patriotic speech. But July 4, 1854 had record high temperatures. Only a handful of people of people marched behind the band. People preferred sitting on their shaded porches licking home-made ice cream. Mr. Macy later moved to New York City, where he organized a parade during a cooler time of year, Thanksgiving."

"Heat won't prevent a Texan from marching in the Fourth of July parade." Mrs. Wood, from Slaton, Texas, interrupted her husband's story. I agreed. In our small Texas town, every man, woman and child was looking forward for the Fourth of July parade to take place in two days. I could hardly wait. I decided to wear my Zulu necklace, a lei of red, white and blue pearls. I pulled my U.S. flag from its dusty garage shelf. My flag was unique. Would I trust it to the West Texas wind? The flag had flown over the Capital in Washington and was given to me by my co-workers at Envoye Travel in 1976 when I became a proud U.S. Citizen. I selected 1976 because of the 200th. birthday of this wonderful country. I let my hand caress each of my friends signatures written on the flag's edge. Little did I know that I wouldn't be around to join in the Fourth of July fun.

At 9 o'clock that night, tired but feeling good as one does after using every muscle in the body, I sank into my bed. My thoughts span around our upcoming Fourth of July celebration. No doubt Dr. Wood planed to make things interesting at the B .B. Q. and pop questions like, "who made the first American flag?" And I will answer, "seamstress Betsy Ross sewed the first American flag. She used 13 stars and stripes to represent the first 13 colonies." And Dr. Wood will blink with his left eye and ask, "How about fireworks?" And I will answer, "The Chinese invented the fireworks. With the noise and the light they hoped to scare off evil demons. Mexicans use fireworks to send messages in to haven." And of course Dr. Wood will ask, "How did the National Anthem come about?" And I will tell him, "During the war of 1812, on September 13, 1814, Francis Scott Key, a Baltimore lawyer, visited the British fleet in Chesapeake Bay to secure the release of Dr. William Beanes, who had been captured after the burning of Washington D. C. The release was secured, but Key was detained on ship over night during the shelling of Fort McHenry, one of the forts defending Baltimore. Watching the licking flames and the horrendous battle Key was convinced that all was lost for the Americans. But, at dawn, though clouds of thick smoke he saw the Star Spangled Banner of the American Flag still flying over the fort. He poured his emotion on the back of an envelope. His poem, "The Star Spangled Banner", quickly attained wide popularity. Soon it was sung to the tune of the old English love and drinking song, "To Anacreon in Heaven," inspired by the Greek writer Anacreon. The song was probably composed by John Stafford Smith, of England, born in 1750. "The Star Spangled Banner" was officially made the National Anthem by Congress in 1931."

I hummed, "Oh say can you see by the dawn's early light, what so proudly we hail'd at the twilight's last gleaming..." Key's emotional lyrics filled my heart with pride to be an American by choice. It unlocked my memories of my life in countries around the world where I worked often as a maid to avoid having to pay for lodging and food in order to add French, Spanish and English, to my German. The first three languages were a must if later on I wished to work at the United Nations as an interpreter. No matter in which one of our Globe's 199 countries I lived, eventually I became homesick for Germany. But then, when I arrived in America, something amazing happened. For the first time in my life I felt at home. More than anyting I wanted to be an American. I wanted to be part of the world's most religious country, the least class conciencious nation on earth, where I could move up, and improve myself, where obsticals were met with compassion, where volunteers where honored. In no time my dreams came true. So hopelessly proud I am to be an American that during my first visit back to Germany my mother told me, "I used to like Americans until you became one. I am tired of hearing you say that everything is better in America."

Shocked I looked at the apple in my hand an said, "Mutti, wonderful apples like the one I am holding in my hand you cannot find in America."

"That's strange." She replied. "That apple is from Oregan, America."

We laughed. My mother had the rare gift to solve differences with humor.

Silently, I thanked my Yankee sponsor for the millionth time for giving me the chance to come to America. And I promised to continue to be a productive citizen and to pay my dues for the right to live in America. Quiertly I asked myself, "what I could contributed to the country I love so much?" Having created many jobs for others since I started my company in 1971 was one thing. And never having accepted as much as a penny from the Government filled me with happiness.

I told my mother, "Come visit us in America."

"America? Is it not too dangerous? " She replied.

And I answered, "Well, you just told me this morning that now that your husband died of a heart attack, you want to die too. So now you might just as well come to America. What do you have to lose?"

"Mensch Sigrid, You are right." My mother replied.

Sooner than I thought, my mother, her seven-year younger sister Hildegard, her partner in adventure, and I, of course, plus six large suitcases left Frankfurt, Germany, one of the most densely populated regions on the planet and headed for one of the least populated. There, in Lubbock, Texas, I had happily married and started Envoye Travel.

Braniff's scenic route between America and Europe was the reason why we choose them. Just flying to America was a great excitement by itself. Gazing down thousands of feet, recognizing oceans, icebergs, the nursery of the Mega Berg that sank the unsinkable Titanic in two and a half hours, spectacular snow-covered mountains, deep blue lakes, endless green fields (the food pantry for the world according to aunt Hilde), and finally the silent high plains home of the world's largest cotton production, with Lubbock, Texas its proud capital.

As our plane begun its descent, I heard my aunt whisper in to my mother's ear. "Six months? How far is Lubbock to a port from which we can take a Caribbean Cruise? Or visit Mexico?"

We smiled when we recognized Dilford, my husband standing among the receiving crowed.

Mother and aunt had never seen a pickup before. Oh, how excited they were. And to ride in one was simply unimaginable Hollywood stuff. "Only in America." My mother smiled as Dilford opened the passenger door for her.

Our adobe home was a thirty-minute drive on a narrow road framed on both shoulder by cottonwood. There was no traffic. Causing Hilde to think this was our private road.

Dilford asked, "What is the German Word for suitcase?" "Koffer" My mother replied.

Calmly Dilford asked, "By the way where are your Koffers?"

"Koffers?" We yelled in desperation. While Dilford turned the truck around to return to the airport.

God must have listened to their despair. How else could this have happened? After all, against any human belief, all 6 bags, there they stood, neatly aligned along the curb.

"This could not have happened in Germany," my mother and aunt cried for joy. Hilde reminded us that she had something special in her Koffer, something she prepared every 4th of July to remind the word that Americans had given liberty and freedom to millions of Germans and Jews from Hitler's socialism.

Halfway on the way back to our home, Dilford stopped on the side of the road. In the west the sky was "fixin" for a radiant, luminous, dazzling, speck table, a feast for the senses, Texas Sunset.

Back at our home, we celebrated with a supper of American hamburgers. Which both ladies ate, according to German custom, with knife and fork.

Dilford and I ate ours with our hands and Dilford saying. "Thank God for Texas."

Years later back in Texas…"riiiing," I reached for the phone knowing instantly who the caller was. 2:30 AM…, the phone call was from Europe, where it was already 9:30 AM, and a civilized hour to call.

"Will you accept a collect call from D.C. Carter?" "Yes Operator. Halo D.C."

"Liebling, I'm in a terrible bind. Please take the next flight over here. Bring all the money you can. My team and I are being held hostage at the Esplanade Hotel. You have to bail us out!"

"But D.C., didn't you tell me that the Yugoslavian Government was paying for all your expenses?"

"Yes, but unfortunately the Minister of Finances is on vacation. And so is his assistant. Nobody in the government of this country is willing to sign for the release of the funds they approved for my research project months ago. Nobody, I mean nobody among these communists will accept any responsibility and sign anything. Meanwhile I'm running up a huge bill. Six people staying at the Esplanade eating three meals a day is expensive. And the hotel will serve us only the most expensive food, because, you guessed it, because we are Americans. My students are getting used to caviar for breakfast."

"Are you kidding?"

"The hotel does not allow us to check out unless we pay our bill."

I promised my desperate husband that I would rush to his rescue, TODAY!. But, where would I get the money? Banks were closed for the long weekend. We don't keep money inside the house. And I, a happily married woman, was nothing like Catherina the Great who always had several thousand in her bedside table with which she silenced her lovers. "How many Travelers Cheques did I have in my Travel Agency?" Desperately my mind counted.

I leapt out of bed and turned on the cold shower. For a few seconds I missed my native Germany where the water stayed ice-cold and invigorating, even in July, not warm like here in Texas. With my skin still wet I struggled into my travel blouse and skirt. I figured that if I hurried I could drive to my office, pick up the Travelers Cheques, catch the 5:45 to DFW, the 7:35 to JFK, the Concord to Paris, the overnight TG V to Geneva and the Orient Express to Zagreb and make it to the Esplanade hotel before D. C and his hungry graduate students eat up an other few hundred dollars worth of caviar.

At my office I ran into a dilemma. I couldn't remember the security alarm code to the entrance to my office. "What year was Henry VIII's first wife born?" I mumbled to myself. I pushed the number 1485. Thank goodness the door opened. Now I had to remember the combination to the safe. I kneeled on the floor, turning the safe's wheel, listened carefully to the clicks again and again. By the time I finally fumbled open the safe, a pair of extra large hands, with the weight of bear-claws grabbed my delicate shoulders from behind. Scared I looked around, staring at a wall of dark blue that wasn't there before. Slowly I lifted my head. Two husky policemen stood behind me. I tried forcing a charming smile and explained, "I am the owner of this Travel Agency."

"Oh yeah?"

I wouldn't be stealing my own money and in the middle of the night, would I? Look, I am in a hurry.

"I bet you are."

"Officers, please believe me, I am on my way to rescue my husband, a biologist studying bats and rats along the Mediterranean shore. I need a fantastic amount of Dinars in order to bail him out."

"Oh yeah?"

Following World War II, the United States sold surplus grain to Yugoslavia and several other countries for payment in their respective currencies. The payments were left in the countries as credits to be used for scientific and cultural exchanges. The Smithsonian manages these funds in what is called the "Excess Currency Program."

The officers looked at each other and rolled their eyes. Obviously, my unusual explanation had made my situation even more suspicious. Silently I called on my Grandmother in heaven for help. She had rescued me out of deep "Sauerkraut" during other disasters. Suddenly a miracle occurred! The phone rang. The police answered.

"We caught the suspect. Strong accent, okay ...."

The officer handed me the receiver and I found myself talking to the National Guardian. Kyle, an employee of the National Guardian had called my office in order to check who had entered my agency without punching 1485. For once, my German accent came in handy. Kyle recognized my accent and assured the police, "The accent is unmistakably that of the owner Sigrid Carter of Envoye Travel."

The police officers apologized profusely. They helped me stuff the travelers cheques into my old, beat-up briefcase and volunteered to escort me to the airport. With sirens wailing and red lights flashing we raced through all the red lights toward the airport. Lucky as always, I made the 5:45 and all of the subsequent connections.

One hundred miles into Yugoslavia I stared through the spotless glass of the train window. Something caught my attention. In every small town our train raced through, people were in the same festive spirit as back home in Texas. Lawns were being groomed, trees pruned, sidewalks swept, and wagons and oxen decorated with wild flowers, flags and streamers.

The moment I stepped off the train in Zagreb my surprise exploded. Brass bands were playing, banners waving and the air smelled of sausages and bar-b-que.

I elbowed my way through a mile-wide, happy crowd. The masses thickened as I came closer to the Esplanade Hotel. Here and there, through an opening in the crowd, I caught glimpses of people dressed in their colorful national costumes, dancing the polka on festively decorated, scaffold stages, built of timber high above the enthusiastic crowd.

"What are you celebrating?" I ask a young girl wearing a crown made of fresh flowers on her long, golden hair. Surprised the little one looked at me. Her big blue eyes sparkled with amazement?

"It's the Fourth of July." She said a bit indignantly. Spontaneously I asked: "Fourth of July? You are celebrating the Fourth of July here in Yugoslavia?" Passionately the girl fired back:

"Fourth of July, Madame, is one of Yugoslavia's most celebrated holidays. It's the birthday of our nation."

"Amazing." I told the girl.

"What's amazing?" She asked.

And I answered, "It's amazing that I get to celebrate Fourth of July after all." Trustingly, she slipped her small hand into mine. Together we walked in the direction of the Esplanade hotel. I told her about my new life in America and how we celebrate Fourth of July. She was totally amazed that Americans celebrate the Fourth of July. With wide eyes she assured me, "It's so nice that children in America don't have to go to school on July Fourth and that you observe our holiday." She squeezed my hand.

At the hotel I had a big laugh. As I stood in line at the cashier's counter I heard the New York accent of the lady in front of me. "Why are all the shops closed?" I was hoping to shop in Zagreb. She bullied.

The hotel clerk answered politely, "Madame, it's July Fourth."

The lady shouted, "Heck, I know that! But, what does that have to do with Yugoslavia?"

"Madame, July Fourth is Independence Day."

"Yes, I know." She hissed impatiently.

He continued, "Today we commemorate Tito's Union of the communist Republics of Yugoslavia. The Union gave us our birthday of our nation, Partisan Day."

The lady must have heard my laugh. She turned around and faced me. "I had the same problem." I sympathized with her and shrugged my shoulders.

And then it was my turn at the cashier's counter.

"Hi, I'm Sigrid Carter from Ransom Canyon, Texas. I'm here to pay the ransom for my husband." I pulled out my Buckingham Palace pen, a gift from Queen Elizabeth at a summer garden party, ready to sign travelers cheques. He gave me the "oh-wunderbar-odlicno-look," and I laughed.

Then he said, "So, you are from Ransom Canyon and you're here to pay a ransom?"

"Yes," I said.

"Unbelievable." He gave me an interrogating look, that made me shiver from my boots to my Texan hat. Another obstacle?

"Freedom tastes better than caviar." A familiar voice said next to me. We hugged. I was so glad to see D.C. He always was so settled and made me feel so safe.

Free at last. That night we danced with the Yugoslavs on the old, historic, cobblestone streets of Zagreb. I imagined myself stepping on the same stones Roman emperors walked. And when the sky exploded with sparkling fireworks we aaahed and ooohed in Croation with the masses and celebrated 2 Fourths of July at the time of 1.

After the Fourth of July the Yugoslavian Government reluctantly agreed to pay my husband the first installment of his research grant. We took the train to Beograd where we were instructed to pick up the cash at the treasury. We carried the fortune in my old ransom briefcase on the Orient Express. On our 12 hour ride back to Zagreb, we didn't dare to look out the window. We were totally oblivious to the spectacular countryside, floating past our window like a movie. Our eyes were riveted to the briefcase. Ironically, it stood among impoverished passengers. What would have happened had anybody on that train known about the fortune just an easy grasp away?

It seemed like eternity until we finally got to spend the Dinars. The money opened the doors to great possibilities. Scientists from the United States of America and Yugoslavia had the chance to conduct research on bats and rodents on both sides of the big pond.

Too unfamiliar with the Med's natural treasures, such as the habitat of one of the world's ten sallest mammals, the Etruscan Pygmy Shrew, less than 2 inches long, weighing not more than a dime, weighing not more than a dime, made me feel stupid, inferior, and well, not up to snuff. Concerned to be a burden, I decided to retreat into my own passion, history, and adventurer. I wrote a note to Dilford explaining my judgement that his expedition would be more successful without me.

At the local Catholic church the mammalogists searched the sidewalks for bat guano that would lead them to the creatures habitat. Feeling useless I escaped into the interior of the church.

Inside I found all pews unoccupied, which confirmed that in order for communism to flourish Christianity and all other relegions had to be quashed. I walked down the main aisle looking at paintngs, St Peter in chains, Christ nailed to the cross, Mary being stoned to death. Suddenly I spotted a young girl. She was crying. She told me that her name was Anfissa. Her father had shot her beloved dog because the dog did not bark at strangers. Anfissa left home and not knowing where to spend the night she entered the church. Looking at the tragic pictures on the wall she was even more scared.

I told her to listened to God. I sang my mother's favorite music, Bach's Air. We stretched out on a wooden bench, darkened by history. Sleep did not come. I cryed with her.

Sunrise did what it always does. It filled us with new energy. The church bell rang and the round, glass window above the althar by the cross started to reveal its unworldly spectacular colors. I walked Anfissa to the convent next door where an older nun invited her for breakfast, a local specialty, asparagus pancakes.

It was time to follow my own destiny. Clearly Dilford needed time to concentrate on his research. This would offer me the oportunity to do something I always wanted to do. After his research we would meet again. And so I traveld by bus to St. Stephan a small island along the spectacular Mediterranean cost . The entire island was one hotel consisting of homes of passed owners. Our yellow bus wound us through a sea of spectacukar wild flowers to the Dubrovnic airport where I purchased a seat on the first flight ready to depart to a destination I had never explored.

The moment our buss stopped at the busy Dubrovnik Airport; an exciting announcement caught my attention that made my heart run faster.

"Flight 11 to Cairo, Egypt is now boarding."

"Wow," I whispered to myself. "Eleven is my lucky number. Could it be that today is the day my wish to go to an airport and board a flight to a country I had never explored is becoming a reality?"

The agent at the *Egypt Air* counter announced in a friendly voice, "Lady, you have the last seat available. It's First Class and highly discounted for productive travel agents like you, according to my computer."

The moment I fastened my seatbelt an ever so attractive flight attendant walked down the aisle informing all passengers,

"Before landing have your visa for your destination ready."

Embarrassed for not carrying a visa, I stared out the window searching diligently the ground for pyramids hundreds of feet below, thousands of years old, with an estimated age of 2686 BCE. All I could see was the golden blanket of the Sahara covering Cairo, while the captain announced,

"In 20,000 some years the Sahara will be green again as it will enter a cooler circle since earth turns on its axis. We are running out of fuel. This is my third, my last attempt to find an opening in this historic sand storm over Cairo."

On the 2 hour and 30-minute flight from Dubrovnik to Cairo the lady seated next to me heard that I had a great 4th of July celebration in the capital of Croatia. She got all excited to meet an American like I. Hurriedly she pulled out her cell phone and showed me pictures of the 4th of July American festivities she attended in Cairo at the campus of the American University AUC in down town Cairo. She invited me to stay with her in her home in Cairo and to meet some of her American friends and to assist me to enter Egypt without the visa I forgot to take with me.

"This is my problem," I laughed. "I forget to take what I need, simply because I always run into somebody that insists to helps me and to want to be my friend. That's particularly true since 1976 when I became an American from being German."

We hugged and agreed, **"create the kind of world you wish to live in."**

Fireworks display over the Potomac River.
The 500-foot tall George Washington Monument in the background. It was started in 1848 and finished in1888.

Fireworks over Washington, D.C., Washington Monument in the foreground.

Fourth of July in Zagreb, Croatia, formerly one of the Autonomous Republics of the Yugoslav Federation.

Unsurprisingly, July 4 celebrations make it all the way to Australia, with Sydney claiming the largest 4th July celebrations in the Southern Hemisphere! Hosted by Sydney Americans, the events take place along the city's famous harbor and includes American DJs and, of course, American food and drink.

Fourth of July celebration in Norway.

The Pacific Ocean. November 15, 1805, Sacagawea, whispering gratitude for the beauty of the Columbia River entering the Pacific Ocean.

24

Her contributions to the world are tremendous.

During her help on Lewis and Clark's Expedition not one person lost its live.

Her favorite sayings were:

- Plant a thought and harvest an act.
- Don't go around believing the world owes you a living.
- I do things for my people. I want them to be proud of me.

Cairo, Egypt United States of America's Embassy

US Consulate General in São Paulo celebrates the Independence Day
of the United States.

Denmark *Rebild National Park* has been holding the largest Fourth of July celebration outside of the United States since 1912. The park's 200 acres were purchased by a group of Danish Americans in 1911 and were deeded to the King and country in 1912 as a permanent memorial to all Danish Americans. As conditions of the gift, the park had to remain undeveloped, open to the public, and available as a space to celebrate American holidays, especially the Fourth of July.

Afterthought

Each Fourth of July celebration rolls around faster these days. And when it arrives we meet it sailing on Lake Ransom Canyon and feasting on hamburgers, B.B.Q. Martha Washington Cherry Pies and cool drinks. The first part of the celebration start at 10 PM on July 3rd . when fireworks explode in the sky above Buffalo Springs. The dark surface of the lake reflects each "Roman Candle, each "Bottle Rocket", and each "Fountain" .. We are looking at 2 skies. Finally we watch what is becoming a new tradition, the peaceful parade of festively decorated boats slowly tracing the shore of our West Texas canyon lake. It seems that each year the fireworks, the parades, the B.B.Q.'s are more spectacular than they were in those early years when a year seemed like eternity and everything was possible.

The Executive Mansion was first painted white in 1817 to hide the scars of its burning by the British. But it had been known before that as the White House- partly because of its gleaming sandstone exterior and partly (so legend has it) because George Washington called it that after his wife's plantation in Virginia. This early view shows it after it had been painted.

The Star Spangled Banner

Lyrics by Francis Scott Key

Music by Stofford Smith

Oh, say, can you see, by the dawn's early light, What so proudly
we hail'd at the twilight's last gleaming?
Whose broad stripes and bright stars, thro' the perilous fight,
O'er the ramparts we watch'd, were so gallantly streaming?
And the rockets' red glare, the bombs bursting in air,
Gave proof thro' the night that our flag was still there.
O say, does that star-spangled banner yet wave O'er the land
of the free and the home of the brave?

On the shore dimly seen thro' the mists of the deep, Where
the foe's haughty host in dread silence reposes, What is that
which the breeze, o'er the towering steep, As it fitfully blows,
half conceals, half discloses?
Now it catches the gleam of the morning's first bea

In full glory reflected, now shines on the stream: 'T is the star-
spangled banner: O, long may it wave O'er the land of the free
and the home of the brave!

And where is that band who so vauntingly swore That the havoc
of war and the battle's confusion A home and a country should
leave us no more?
Their blood has wash'd out their foul footsteps' pollution. No
refuge could save the hireling and slave From the terror of
flight or the gloom of the grave: And the star-spangled banner

31

in triumph doth wave O'er the land of the free and the home of the brave.

O, thus be it ever when freemen shall stand, Between their lov'd homes and the war's desolation;

Blest with vict'ry and peace, may the heav'n-rescued land Praise the Pow'r that hath made and preserv'd us as a nation!

Then conquer we must, when our cause is just,

And this be our motto: "In God is our trust" And the star-spangled banner in triumph shall wave O'er the land of the free and the home of the brave!

Sigrid and Dilford Carter enjoying a cruise complements of American Express. Envoye Travel and team of 40 travel agents placed among the 50 best American Express Affiliated Travel Agencies in the U.S.

Author, Sigrid Carter came to the United States in 1960, at age 23. In 1964 she and three German girl friends back packed from Aspen, Colorado to the Tierra del Fuego. It was on this 18 months trek, that she met Dilford Carter, her future husband, a biologist from Texas A&M. Sigrid worked for her husbands expedition helping him with his research in the Amazon rain forest. The couple married in 1967, and Sigrid started her career as a travel agent, in College Station, Texas. In 1971 Dilford accepted a position as Associate Dean of the Graduate School at Texas Tech University in Lubbock, Texas. Sigrid opened Envoye Travel. It is today Lubbock's oldest Travel Agency. Sigrid is an adventures, a world traveler, a cancer survivor and an author of *Amazing Woman, Travel Like a Millionare Without Being One* and *A Christmas Tale for Each Advent Day*. She conveys an infectious zest for life. She is on a weekly call in radio talk show, "The Big Ed Show". She starts her day with kayaking and yoga on her boat dock and a dance to celebrate life. What a woman. Thank you Sigrid for allowing us to become acquainted with you and Dilford.

- Judy and David Conejo, Ransom Canyon.

Author Sigrid Carter born in Essen Germany in 1936 shown here in Lubbock, Texas celebrating her first July 4th. 1976. Ready to make America proud of her, she started her own business, Envoye Travel & Cruise, creating countless jobs and tax payers.

When I was just a little girl growing up in World War II Germany, my Grandfather asked me,

"Sigrid, when you grew up, what do you want to be?"

"Grandpa," I replied, **"When I grow up I want to be an American!"**

Printed in the United States
by Baker & Taylor Publisher Services